TENNESSEE POST OFFICE MURAL GUIDEBOOK

DAVID W. GATES JR.

POST OFFICE FANS
Crystal Lake, Illinois

Copyright © 2020 David W. Gates Jr.
1st Edition

Tennessee Post Office Mural Guidebook / David W. Gates Jr.

ISBN: 978-1-970088-06-9 (Paperback)
ISBN: 978-1-970088-07-6 (EPUB)
ISBN: 978-1-970088-08-3 (PDF)

All rights reserved. No part of this publication may be reproduced, stored, or transmitted in any form or by any means, electronic, mechanical, photocopying, recording, scanning, or otherwise, without written permission from the publisher. It is illegal to copy this book, post it to a website, or distribute it by any other means without permission.

David W. Gates Jr. asserts the moral right to be identified as the author of this work.

Neither David W. Gates Jr. nor the publisher are responsible for the persistence or accuracy of URLs for external or third-party Internet websites referred to in this publication and do not guarantee that any content on such websites is, or will remain, accurate or appropriate.

Designations used by companies to distinguish their products are often claimed as trademarks. All brand names and product names used in this book and on its cover are trade names, service marks, trademarks and registered trademarks of their respective owners. Neither the publishers nor the book are associated with any product or vendor mentioned in this book. None of the companies referenced within the book have endorsed the book.

To contact the publisher:

Post Office Fans
PO Box 11
Crystal Lake, IL 60039
Phone: 815-206-8405
info@postofficefans.com • www.postofficefans.com

Cover and text design by John Reinhardt Book Design
Front cover photo: Lenoir City Post Office, Lenoir City, Tennessee

Contents

Post Office Location Map v
Preface vii
Introduction 1

Bolivar 3
Camden 4
Chattanooga 5
Clarksville 7
Clinton 8
Columbia 9
Crossville 11
Dayton 12
Decherd 13
Dickson 14
Dresden 15
Gleason 16
Greeneville 17
Jefferson City 18
Johnson City 19
La Follette 20
Lenoir City 21
Lewisburg 22
Lexington 23
Livingston 24

Manchester. 25
McKenzie. 26
Mount Pleasant 27
Nashville 28
Newport 29
Ripley 30
Rockwood 31
Sweetwater 32

Summary. 33
About the Author 35
Upcoming Books 37
Other Titles by the Publisher 39

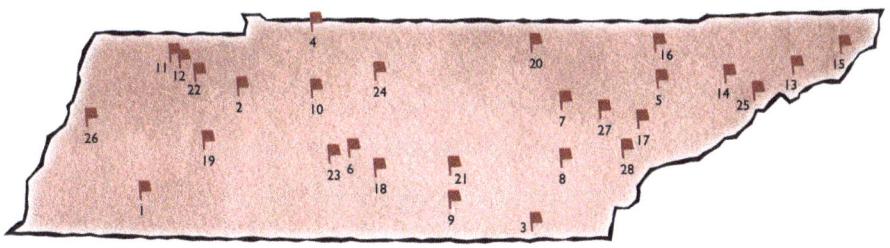

Tennessee Post Office Murals

1. Bolivar
2. Camden
3. Chattanooga
4. Clarksville (former)
5. Clinton (former)
6. Columbia (former)
7. Crossville
8. Dayton (former)
9. Decherd
10. Dickson
11. Dresden
12. Gleason
13. Greeneville (former)
14. Jefferson City
15. Johnson City (former)
16. La Follette (former)
17. Lenoir City
18. Lewisburg (former)
19. Lexington (former)
20. Livingston
21. Manchester (former)
22. McKenzie (former)
23. Mount Pleasant
24. Nashville
25. Newport (former)
26. Ripley
27. Rockwood
28. Sweetwater

~ v ~

PREFACE

THE STATISTICS I'VE READ report there are somewhere between 1,100 and 1,400 works of art located in public post offices nationwide. Since I've been unable to verify these statistics, I've made it my mission to find out exactly how many exist and view them all.

What began for me as a casual interest in a photographic subject soon became a deep fascination with the history and presence of a unique moment in American culture and art. Before creating this guidebook, I visited hundreds of post offices and spoke to dozens of people across the U.S., and I realized we were united in our enthusiasm for keeping the stories of this art alive and available for the American public.

The guidebook you are viewing today is an account of all 28 of Tennessee's New Deal post office murals. I encourage you to visit one of these post offices in Tennessee or seek out one in your own state. To learn about this special art is to learn about the continuing American journey.

When I initially researched the post offices in Tennessee, I discovered the original *Tennessee Post Office Murals* book by Mr. Howard Hull. Since completing the *Wisconsin Post Office Mural Guidebook*, I found it fitting to create one for Tennessee. This led to the book you are holding today. It provides a quick reference of the New Deal murals in Tennessee.

There are no images of the murals in this book. It is meant solely as a reference to the buildings in Tennessee. This guide provides the: address, title of the work, artist, and status. I've found having a book like this makes for a handy reference and personal checklist.

I've created this guidebook for your benefit, in case you find yourself needing the same checklist as you travel and discover each building and mural. I hope this book brings you enjoyment and knowledge. There is no need to scour multiple sources to find the status of each one. I've done the work for you. Print it out or download it to your mobile device to bring with you on your next post office visit.

Thank you,

David W. Gates Jr.

Introduction

FROM 1934–1943, fascinating murals and various forms of art were commissioned and installed in public buildings under the United States Treasury Department's Section of Painting and Sculpture, later renamed the Section of Fine Arts.

My research revealed two reasons for installing art in post offices. The first was to bring light and hope to a country gripped by the Great Depression, and the second was to employ artists during this difficult time.

Anonymous competitions were held to select artists for new federal buildings that were being constructed during this time. Commissions paid to the artists were approximately one percent of the congressional appropriation to construct the new post office buildings.

This informative book lists all the post offices in Tennessee that received artwork. It gives you a quick reference to the New Deal post office murals in Tennessee. It includes:

- Full address
- Artist
- Title
- Medium
- Status
- Link for further reading

While this short guide does not provide images of the actual art, it does provide you a quick reference to the post office art in Tennessee. Although the title of the book says "mural," I use that term inclusively. Tennessee is lucky in that they also received art commissioned in mediums such as wood carvings, terra cotta, bronze, and aluminum.

Bolivar

Address: 118 E. Market St., Bolivar, Tennessee 38008

Artist: Carl Nyquist

Title: *Picking Cotton*

Medium: Oil on canvas (mural)

Status: The Bolivar post office is still an active, operating facility, and the mural can be viewed by interested members of the public. It resides in the lobby on the wall above the postmaster's door.

Web: www.postofficefans.com/bolivar-tennessee-post-office/

CAMDEN

ADDRESS: 81 N. Forrest Ave., Camden, Tennessee 38320

ARTIST: John H. Fyfe

TITLE: *Mail Delivery to Tranquility — The first post office in Benton County*

MEDIUM: Oil on canvas (mural)

STATUS: The Camden post office is still an active, operating facility, and the mural can be viewed by interested members of the public. It resides in the lobby on the wall above the postmaster's door.

WEB: www.postofficefans.com/camden-tennessee-post-office/

CHATTANOOGA
Post Office and Courthouse

ADDRESS: 910 Georgia Ave., Chattanooga, Tennessee 37402

ARTIST: Leopold Scholz

TITLE: *The Mail Carrier*

MEDIUM: Silver plated bronze (sculpture)

STATUS: The Chattanooga post office and courthouse is still an active, operating facility. It's known as the Joel W. Solomon Federal Building. The bronze sculpture resides in the lobby near the staircase and can be viewed by interested members of the public during business hours.

WEB: www.postofficefans.com/chattanooga-tennessee-post-office-and-courthouse/

Chattanooga
Post Office and Courthouse (cont'd)

Address: 910 Georgia Ave., Chattanooga, Tennessee 37402

Artist: Hilton Leech

Title: *Allegory of Chattanooga*

Medium: Oil on canvas (mural)

Status: The mural resides in a courtroom and is not easily accessible to the public.

Web: www.postofficefans.com/chattanooga-tennessee-post-office-and-courthouse/

Clarksville

ADDRESS: 116 N. 2nd Street, Clarksville, Tennessee 37040

ARTIST: F. Luis Mora

TITLES: *Abundance of Today* and *Arrival of Col. John Donaldson*

MEDIUM: Oil on Canvas (murals)

STATUS: No longer a post office, this building is occupied by the Federal Bureau of Investigation. Research and rumors indicate the murals have been destroyed. There is one completed mural image at the National Archives that I'm aware of.

WEB: www.postofficefans.com/former-clarksville-tennessee-post-office/

Clinton

ADDRESS: 362 N. Main St., Clinton, Tennessee 37716

ARTIST: Horace Day

TITLE: *Farm and Factory*

MEDIUM: Tempera (mural)

STATUS: The mural no longer resides in the original building shown here. It was moved to the newer post office building on N. Charles G. Seivers Blvd. It resides in the lobby and is accessible to members of the public interested in viewing it.

WEB: www.postofficefans.com/former-clinton-tennessee-post-office/

Columbia
Post Office and Courthouse

Address: 815 South Garden Street, Columbia, Tennessee 38401

Artist: Henry Billings

Title: *Maury County Landscape*

Medium: Oil on canvas (mural)

Status: The Columbia post office no longer operates at this location; however, the courthouse is still an active, operating facility, the mural resides in the lobby on the first floor, and is not easily accessible.

Web: www.postofficefans.com/former-columbia-tennessee-post-office-and-courthouse/

Columbia

Post Office and Courthouse (cont'd)

Address: 815 South Garden Street, Columbia, Tennessee 38401

Artist: Sidney Waugh

Title: *American Eagle*

Medium: Marble (sculpture)

Status: The Columbia post office no longer operates at this location; however, the courthouse is still an active, operating facility. The mural resides in the lobby on the first floor, and is not easily accessible. The stone eagle sculpture resides on the exterior top of the building as shown in the photo.

Web: www.postofficefans.com/former-columbia-tennessee-post-office-and-courthouse/

CROSSVILLE

ADDRESS: 2 South Main St., Crossville, Tennessee 38555

ARTIST: Marion Greenwood

TITLE: *The Partnership of Man and Nature*

MEDIUM: Oil on canvas (mural)

STATUS: The mural no longer resides in the original building shown here. It was moved to the newer post office building on Old Jamestown Hwy. It resides in the lobby and is accessible to members of the public interested in viewing it.

WEB: www.postofficefans.com/former-crossville-tennessee-post-office/

Dayton

ADDRESS: 400 Main St., Dayton, Tennessee 37321

ARTIST: Bertram Hartman

TITLE: *View from Johnson's Bluff*

MEDIUM: Oil on canvas (mural)

STATUS: The post office no longer operates out of this location. However, the mural still resides here. The building is currently home to Dayton Electric and Water. The mural is in the lobby and is accessible to members of the public interested in viewing it during business hours.

WEB: www.postofficefans.com/former-dayton-tennessee-post-office/

Decherd

Address: 305 E. Main St., Decherd, Tennessee 37324

Artist: Enea Biafora

Title: *News on the Job*

Medium: Wood (carving)

Status: The Decherd post office is still an active, operating facility, and the wood carving can be viewed by interested members of the public. It resides in the lobby on the wall above the postmaster's door.

Web: www.postofficefans.com/decherd-tennessee-post-office/

Dickson

ADDRESS: 215 W. College St., Dickson, Tennessee 37055

ARTIST: Edwin Boyd Johnson

TITLE: *People of the Soil*

MEDIUM: Fresco (mural)

STATUS: The post office no longer operates out of this location. However, the mural still resides here. According to my knowledge and research, the building is privately owned. The mural is in the lobby and is NOT accessible to members of the public. The mural was painted directly into the plaster wall and may have been too costly to remove when the building was sold.

WEB: www.postofficefans.com/former-dickson-tennessee-post-office/

Dresden

Address: 122 Maple St., Dresden, Tennessee 38225

Artist: Minetta Good

Title: *Retrospection*

Medium: Oil on canvas (mural)

Status: The Dresden post office is still an active, operating facility, and the mural can be viewed by interested members of the public. It resides in the lobby on the wall above the postmaster's door.

Web: www.postofficefans.com/dresden-tennessee-post-office/

Gleason

Address: 100 N. Cedar St., Gleason, Tennessee 38229

Artist: Anne Poor

Title: *Gleason Agriculture*

Medium: Oil on canvas (mural)

Status: The Gleason post office is still an active, operating facility, and the mural can be viewed by interested members of the public. It resides in the lobby on the wall above the postmaster's door.

Web: www.postofficefans.com/gleason-tennessee-post-office/

GREENEVILLE
Post Office and Courthouse

Address: 101 W. Summer St., Greeneville, Tennessee 37743

Artist: William Zorach

Titles: *Man Power* and *Natural Resources*

Medium: Wood (reliefs)

Status: The wood reliefs no longer reside in the original building shown here. They were moved to the newer courthouse building on Depot St. The reliefs are located in a courtroom and NOT easily accessible to members of the public.

Web: www.postofficefans.com/former-greeneville-tennessee-post-office/

JEFFERSON CITY

ADDRESS: 101 E. Old Andrew Johnson Hwy., Jefferson City, Tennessee 37760

ARTIST: Charles Child

TITLE: *Great Smokies and Tennessee Farms*

MEDIUM: Oil on canvas (mural)

STATUS: The Jefferson City post office is still an active, operating facility, and the mural can be viewed by interested members of the public. It resides in the lobby on the wall above the postmaster's door.

WEB: www.postofficefans.com/jefferson-city-tennessee-post-office/

Johnson City

Address: 338 E. Main St., Johnson City, Tennessee 37601

Artist: Wendell Jones

Title: *Farmer Family*

Medium: Oil on canvas (mural)

Status: The mural no longer resides in the original building shown here. It was moved to the Charles C. Sherrod Library on the campus of Eastern Tennessee University. The mural is on display in the testing center room and is accessible to members of the public.

Web: www.postofficefans.com/former-johnson-city-tennessee-post-office/

La Follette

Address: 119 S. Tennessee Ave., La Follette, Tennessee 37766

Artist: Dahlov Ipcar

Title: *On the Shores of the Lake*

Medium: Oil on canvas (mural)

Status: The mural no longer resides in the original building shown here. It was moved to the newer post office building on Central Ave. The mural is on display in the lobby and is accessible to members of the public during business hours.

Web: www.postofficefans.com/former-la-follette-tennessee-post-office/

LENOIR CITY

ADDRESS: 217 E. Broadway St., Lenoir City, Tennessee 37771

ARTIST: David Stone Martin

TITLE: *Electrification*

MEDIUM: Oil on canvas (mural)

STATUS: The Lenoir City post office is still an active, operating facility, and the mural can be viewed by interested members of the public. It resides in the lobby on the wall above the postmaster's door.

WEB: www.postofficefans.com/lenoir-city-tennessee-post-office/

LEWISBURG

ADDRESS: 121 S. 1st. Ave., Lewisburg, Tennessee 37091

ARTIST: John H. R. Pickett

TITLE: *Coming 'Round the Mountain*

MEDIUM: Oil on canvas (mural)

STATUS: The mural no longer resides in the original building shown here. It was moved to the newer post office building on Commerce St. The mural is on display in the lobby and is accessible to members of the public.

WEB: www.postofficefans.com/former-lewisburg-tennessee-post-office/

Lexington

Address: 26 S. Broad St., Lexington, Tennessee 38351

Artist: Grace Greenwood (Ames)

Title: *Progress of Power*

Medium: Oil on canvas (mural)

Status: No longer a post office, this building is occupied by the Beech River Heritage Museum. The mural is on display above the former postmaster's office door in the lobby. It is accessible to members of the public during museum hours.

Web: www.postofficefans.com/former-lexington-tennessee-post-office/

LIVINGSTON

ADDRESS: 105 S. Court Sq., Livingston, Tennessee 38570

ARTIST: Margaret Covey Chisholm

TITLE: *The Newcomers*

MEDIUM: Oil on canvas (mural)

STATUS: The Livingston post office is still an active, operating facility, and the mural can be viewed by interested members of the public. It resides in the lobby on the wall above the postmaster's door.

WEB: www.postofficefans.com/livingston-tennessee-post-office/

MANCHESTER

ADDRESS: 200 N. Spring St., Manchester, Tennessee 37355

ARTIST: Minna Citron

TITLE: *Horse Swapping Day*

MEDIUM: Oil on canvas (mural)

STATUS: The mural no longer resides in the original building shown here. It was moved to the newer post office building on Hillsboro Blvd. The mural is on display behind the retail counter. It is only viewable during business hours.

WEB: www.postofficefans.com/former-manchester-tennessee-post-office/

McKenzie

ADDRESS: 640 N. Main St., McKenzie, Tennessee 38201

ARTIST: Karl Oberteuffer

TITLE: *Early U.S. Post Village*

MEDIUM: Oil on canvas (mural)

STATUS: The mural no longer resides in the original building shown here. It was moved to the newer post office building on Highland Dr. The mural is on display behind the retail counter. It is only viewable during business hours.

WEB: www.postofficefans.com/former-mckenzie-tennessee-post-office/

Mount Pleasant

ADDRESS: 201 N. Main St., Mount Pleasant, Tennessee 38474

ARTIST: Eugene Higgins

TITLE: *Early Settlers Entering Mount Pleasant*

MEDIUM: Oil on canvas (mural)

STATUS: The Mount Pleasant post office is still an active, operating facility, and the mural can be viewed by interested members of the public. It resides in the lobby on the wall above the postmaster's door.

WEB: www.postofficefans.com/mount-pleasant-tennessee-post-office/

NASHVILLE

ADDRESS: 901 Broadway, Nashville, Tennessee 37202

ARTIST: Belle Kinney

TITLE: *Portrait Bust of Admiral Albert Gleaves*

MEDIUM: Portrait (bust)

STATUS: The post office does maintain a small operating facility here, However, the bronze bust was moved to the State Capitol and can be viewed by interested members of the public.

WEB: www.postofficefans.com/former-nashville-tennessee-post-office/

Newport

ADDRESS: 219 E. Broadway St., Newport, Tennessee 37821

ARTIST: Minna Citron

TITLE: *TVA Power*

MEDIUM: Oil on canvas (murals)

STATUS: The murals no longer reside in the original building shown here. They were moved to the Newport Community Center on Cosby Highway. The murals are located in the second-floor museum. They are only viewable during very limited volunteer hours or by appointment.

WEB: www.postofficefans.com/former-newport-tennessee-post-office/

Ripley

Address: 117 E. Jackson Ave., Ripley, Tennessee 38063

Artist: Marguerite Zorach

Title: *Autumn*

Medium: Oil on canvas (mural)

Status: The Ripley post office is still an active, operating facility, and the mural can be viewed by interested members of the public. It resides in the lobby on the wall above the postmaster's door.

Web: www.postofficefans.com/ripley-tennessee-post-office/

Rockwood

Address: 340 W. Rockwood St., Rockwood, Tennessee 37854

Artist: Christian Heinrich

Title: *Wild Life*

Medium: Terra cotta (relief)

Status: The Rockwood post office is still an active, operating facility, and the relief can be viewed by interested members of the public. It resides in the lobby on the wall above the postmaster's door.

Web: www.postofficefans.com/rockwood-tennessee-post-office/

Sweetwater

Address: 701 N. Main St., Sweetwater, Tennessee 37874

Artist: Thelma Martin

Title: *Wild Boar Hunt*

Medium: Egg tempera (mural)

Status: The Sweetwater post office is still an active, operating facility, and the mural can be viewed by interested members of the public. It resides in the lobby on the wall above the postmaster's door.

Web: www.postofficefans.com/sweetwater-tennessee-post-office/

Summary

I CREATED THIS BOOK as a reference for myself, as well as for those who are interested in these wonderful buildings and works of art. My goal is to provide you a valuable reference list of the buildings in Tennessee that house murals. For more information about each one and to participate in the discussion of any of the buildings or art, please visit www.postofficefans.com.

This book contains all the post offices in Tennessee that had art installed as a part of the New Deal. This book provides notes on the location and accessibility and status of the art. I've personally visited and photographed each building. Please note this is not a complete list of all the post office buildings constructed in Tennessee during the New Deal, only the ones that housed art.

I welcome your comments, suggestions, or feedback. You may reach me through the following social channels. Of course, I also welcome mail through the United States Postal Service.

About the Author

DAVID W. GATES JR. is a post office enthusiast and author who has traveled thousands of miles nationwide in search of historic post offices buildings and art.

He blogs about his work at:

www.postofficefans.com

Although the murals have been around for more than 86 years, David discovered how often these are overlooked. Join David in his quest to visit them all.

He lives in Crystal Lake, IL with his wife, son and two cats. When not photographing and documenting post offices, he can be found cooking, baking, hiking, or involved in do-it-yourself projects at home, not necessarily all at once and not necessarily in that order.

Upcoming Books

Tennessee Post Office Murals
by David W. Gates Jr.

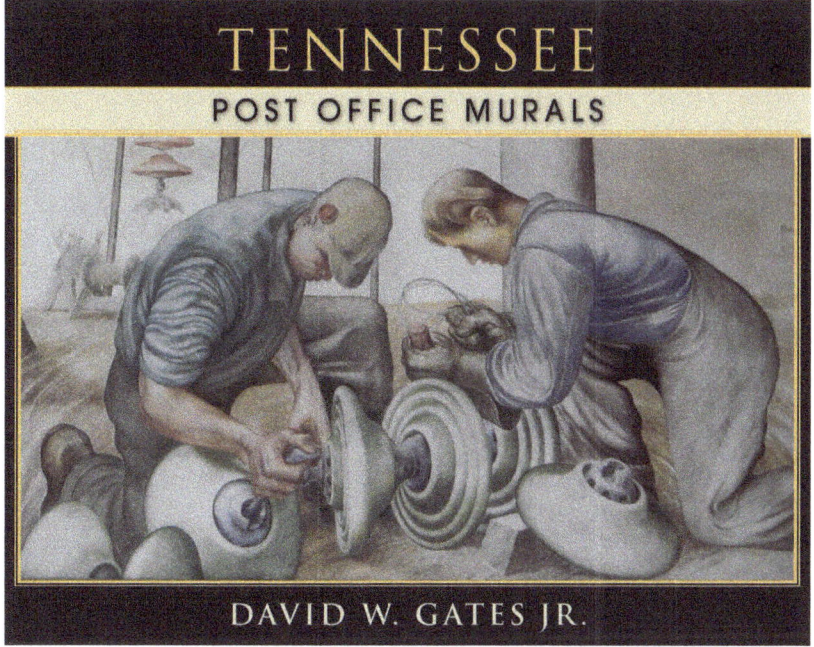

Tennessee Post Office Murals dives deeper into the particulars, including how the murals were developed by the artists. The correspondence and letters created during this time provide a fascinating glimpse of our nation's history. The author's research reveals the efforts of the government and local communities during this time.

Not every community was thrilled with the idea of the subject matter or money spent on artwork for their local post office building.

The murals were installed in small communities throughout Tennessee on purpose. They were meant to bring significant art to everyday Americans. This is public art and the post office was the most public of places during this era. One hundred twenty-five full color images celebrate these wonderful pieces of art as they exist today. Fifty-six color images of the buildings and cornerstones give the reader a sense of being there. ***Tennessee Post Office Murals*** is the armchair traveler's guide to post office murals in Tennessee.

If you have enjoyed this book or found it useful,
please share it with your family, friends,
and social media followers.

Other Titles By The Publisher

Wisconsin Post Office Murals
by David W. Gates Jr.

ISBN: 978-1-970088-00-7 (Paperback)
ISBN: 978-1-970088-01-4 (EPUB)
ISBN: 978-1-970088-02-1 (PDF)

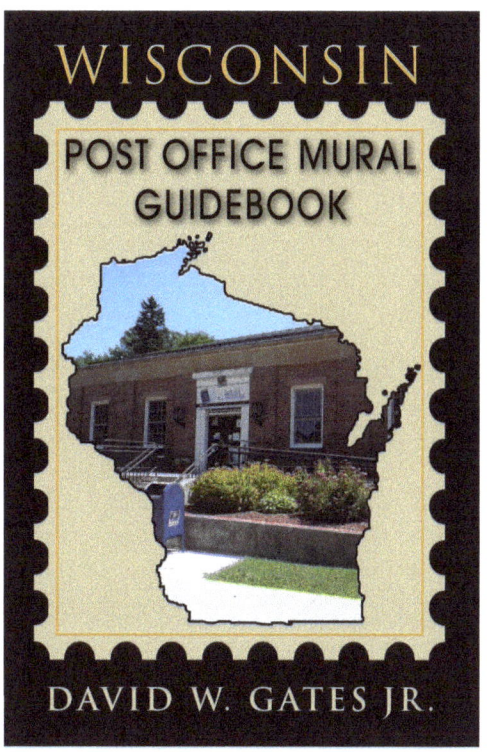

WISCONSIN POST OFFICE MURAL GUIDEBOOK

by David W. Gates Jr.

ISBN: 978-1-970088-09-0 (Paperback)
ISBN: 978-1-970088-10-6 (EPUB)
ISBN: 978-1-970088-11-3 (PDF)

www.ingramcontent.com/pod-product-compliance
Lightning Source LLC
Chambersburg PA
CBHW061212070526
44583CB00025B/3221